A. ACCILI

Antonia's Italy – Walking Tours of Florence
A Guide to Its Art, Food & Fun

Copyright © 2022 by A. Accili

All rights reserved. No part of this publication may be reproduced, stored or transmitted in any form or by any means, electronic, mechanical, photocopying, recording, scanning, or otherwise without written permission from the publisher. It is illegal to copy this book, post it to a website, or distribute it by any other means without permission.

A. Accili asserts the moral right to be identified as the author of this work.

A. Accili has no responsibility for the persistence or accuracy of URLs for external or third-party Internet Websites referred to in this publication and does not guarantee that any content on such Websites is, or will remain, accurate or appropriate.

Designations used by companies to distinguish their products are often claimed as trademarks. All brand names and product names used in this book and on its cover are trade names, service marks, trademarks and registered trademarks of their respective owners. The publishers and the book are not associated with any product or vendor mentioned in this book. None of the companies referenced within the book have endorsed the book.

Third edition

*This book was professionally typeset on Reedsy.
Find out more at reedsy.com*

This book is dedicated to my paternal great grandparents who braved a passage in steerage to arrive in Trail and Spokane in the early 1900's. Grit, savvy, an honorable work ethic and love of family, allowed them to erect businesses and lives setting examples for the generations that followed. None of them returned to Italy. My loving Nonnie Notti Amicarella encouraged me to study in Italy to see where our family began. She insisted I reconnect with family left behind. Nonnie was my spark.

"Everything about Florence seems to be colored with a mild violet, like diluted wine."

-Henry James, writer, in a letter dated 1869

Contents

1	Introduction	1
2	Pre-Trip Planning in a Post Covid World	11
3	Getting Around in Florence	20
4	Where to Stay	29
5	An Aperitivo On A Rooftop After a Walk	32
6	La Famiglia - The Medici	35
7	Top 5 Walks	37
8	Florentine Food	89
9	Top 14 Places to Eat	94
10	Top 4 Authentic Artisanal Gelato Shops	107
11	Grazie Mille!	110
12	Let's Hear From You!	111
13	Resources	112
About the Author		114

One

Introduction

Welcome - Benvenuto!

F*irenze, The Arno River*

***

"*Firenze mi fe'!*" - Florence made me - (Derived from Dante)

I ADORE Florence! I lived in this magnificent jewel my junior year of college at Gonzaga University over 40 years ago. That year changed me. Forever. As Dante wrote in the Divine Comedy, *"Siena mi fe'!* (Siena made me!) Well, Florence made me.

Thanks to my great grandmother's nudging, Florence became my home, my destiny, when I was 20. Life changing events occurred for me in this majestic city. The journey began in Florence with new family

Introduction

connections and a year among the Italian people and legendary culture.

I met my cousin, Mario, in Florence, one month after I arrived on Italian soil. He drove 5 hours from his home in Como to Florence to meet me, immediately, the day after I phoned him and introduced myself. To this day, I am certain he did not understand a thing I was saying, or more aptly put, was TRYING to say, during our first telephone call. But he knew from the little college Italian I could speak, that we were expected to meet when I mentioned our Uncle Ermete.

We did. I drew the family tree. His eyes lit up and... *allora!* Mario knew we were family! All doubts or suspicions instantly vanished. We stuck to pen and paper drawings and loads of hand gesturing and smiles for the rest of the afternoon to communicate. Mario proceeded to enthusiastically arrange for me to take the train to Abruzzo one week later to meet the rest of the family. He returned to Como that same afternoon. What was to follow, was sweet and ever lasting.

There had been little physical contact for 80 years between those who remained in Italy and those who immigrated to Trail, British Colombia and Spokane, Washington. My great grandparents left Abruzzo and Calabria to forge new lives in the early 1900's. The exception to the absence of contact was a one day visit in the 1950's from my Uncle Ed, and a 3 hour visit with my Aunt Jojo who passed through the village of Acciano in the early 1960's. I arrived 20 years later in Acciano in glorious Abruzzo. (Over the last 40 years, others in the family, from the US, have made the journey.)

On my first visit, thanks to Mario's planning, I was greeted by a lively village band (all related to me) who were making their way from the top of the mountain to the bottom while playing their trombones and

Antonia's Italy - Walking Tours of Florence

symbols, when I ran in to them on the road as I was making my way up the mountain to the town. They joyfully and loudly welcomed me with warm embraces, continuous music and endless smiles. I was welcomed with the utmost kindness, old world hospitality and outpouring of love, led by my cousin, Angelina. **I felt "at home," instantly.**

One of the clearest memories of that first week in Acciano was the initial conversation with my dear Angelina at dinner. She hosted me during that week with her *gentile* husband, Amerino, and two *simpatiche* daughters, Gemmina and Pierina. I could not really understand much of what she was saying since for the most part, she spoke in the rich dialect of the village. But, Angelina managed to make it very clear, she was deeply grateful for her Aunt Filomena's gifts sent from Spokane to her family during the war. Her eyes literally sparkled as she shared her stories.

I had no idea that my Nonnie (her Aunt) sent gifts to our Italian relatives during WWII. My cousins eagerly explained, with lots of hand gestures and raised eyebrows, that there had been some letters and photos exchanged during WWII. The photos they received from abroad were treated as precious gifts. They were a tangible connection to the family in Canada and America who were dearly missed. She revealed that most of the photos were burned when the Nazi's arrived in the village, 35 years prior. They rounded up nearly all of the resident's personal and sentimental items from their homes, including photos, and burned them all in the piazza as they left Italy and returned to Germany, once Mussolini had been hung and Italy changed its alliance. A few photos survived that had been stored in cookie tins. They showed me all of them, one at a time, with great care.

There were more gifts from America to add to the letters and photos.

Introduction

There were care packages of clothing, wrapped in softened flour sacks from US Macaroni, by my Nonnie. The pasta factory was started by my great grandfather, Giovanni Amicarella. He was born in Acciano and left for America at 13 years of age. But it was Nonnie, who was from Grimaldi, Calabria, who voluntarily and happily, helped her husband's family survive the perils of the war. Nonnie cleverly hid money sewn in to the hems of the dresses and pants, placed in these bundles, sewed them up into a tight parcel and mailed them to Italy to Angelina's family. The clothing kept them warm and the money allowed them to avoid starvation.

Angelina also showed me her wedding photo that first night in Acciano. She was wearing a lovely, perfectly pressed suit from one of the care packages. She explained how honored she was to be wearing this suit from Nonnie, for her *"matrimonio."* As we sat around the table, Angelina's brother, Diamante, brought out a well-worn felt hat from his back pocket to show me. It was visibly thread bare. He explained to me that he had been wearing that hat for over 40 years, since he was a young boy and, "it was his favorite possession." It too had been in a parcel. I found out later, the hat had belonged to my Nonnie's son, when he was a boy, before it ended up in the bundle for Acciano.

I recall sitting at that table, looking at my cousins' beautiful faces and feeling so grateful that I was with them, in Acciano, the village where three of my great grandparents were born and raised. I never met any of them. But I was quietly thinking to myself if I could write them a postcard, it would include, "I made it back to your home *bisnonni*. It's absolutely beautiful here in these soaring, rugged mountains."

But it was the affect that Nonnie's thoughtfulness had on the lives of my cousins who lived 8000 miles away, that touched me deeply. She brought them hope during a dark, unspeakable period of our history. This first visit was a significant event in my life and it all began in Florence with *caro* Mario's arrival from Como.

Forty plus years later, I still get very emotional when I think back to that first encounter with my cousins, especially since most of them have passed. Like so many villages in Italy, the elderly have died and their children have left for the larger cities to secure work. I still return to Acciano and enjoy the time that is offered to visit and to learn about the experiences of those who remain. And when I am home, I think about when it might be possible to return again, while the sweet memories of those who have gone before me, comfort and sustain me.

That year abroad in Florence, I also fell in love with Italy's natural and historical wonders and the poetic language of Dante. Thanks to many including my Italian cousins, my remarkable and inspiring art history teacher, Dr. Mercedes Carrara, 13 year old language partner Bianca Fama and her family, the Gelli family who lovingly cared for us in our pensione, and the local Florentines, I was inspired to learn Italian. Italian propelled me forward…to live… *Italian style*, and I embraced it. Communicating in Italian opened doors that only language can do…to Italy's people and her culture. And, best of all, I discovered that when I speak this language, *I feel it*, that is, I am very happy and joyful, moving my mouth and my hands.

For the last four decades I have been traveling back to visit my cousins and to experience the magic of Bella Italia, and all its riches, all over again and again. I can never get enough of Firenze (or Abruzzo.)

I have watched Florence change as world travelers discover her splendors. Globalization has left its mark. But even with the shoulder-to-

Introduction

shoulder crowds, it is still one of my favorite places.

And for the last 15 years, I have been fortunate to travel to a number of other unexplored cities in Italy with my brilliant Italian teacher, Wendy Walsh. Her language trips re-energized my curiosity and love for Italian. And through her courses and memorable trips, I have met fellow students who have become my dearest friends, all because of our mutual love for this beautiful country and *everything* about it - the fabulous, the nutty, the challenging, the upsetting, the trains, the art and music, the artisans, the history, fresh and flavorful food, morning stops at the bars, the baristas, wine and aperitifs, the bakeries, the fashion, the artisans, the cars, the cobblestone streets and architecture, the piazzas, the lines, the Cyprus trees, acres of sunflowers, the beaches, vineyards, soaring Apennines and Dolomites, the islands, the coffee, olive groves and plentiful fruit trees, the carefree children, sounds of church bells, the hand and body expressions, the idioms and the grammar, the story telling manner of speaking, the evening passeggiata, the smell of the old earth, the cultural nuances - **all of it!**

* * *

I am compiling these walking tours and suggestions to share my home away from home with you my fellow travelers, so that you too can experience some of Italy's allure, beauty and historical significance in our collective humanity, at YOUR own pace.

We will begin with Florence. My plan is to share some of the knowledge learned through the Gonzaga program, infused with lessons from graduate school and recently, insights through Wendy's immersion trips. This pocket guide, unlike this introduction, is condensed so as not to overwhelm you with fluff and to help you manage your time.

This content is meant to augment your experiences with the real experts, the licensed guides of Florence. The Italians take great pride in their history. There's no better way to see that in action than the arduous program in place to issue licenses for tour guides. To become a guide, one must take a rigorous course of study and pass a very challenging test unique to each region of Italy.

There are 20 regions in Italy. Each has its own rich, complex history. Only the privileged few who pass the exam will become an official guide. I highly recommend you hire a licensed guide in most towns you visit in Bella Italia. The local guides know about recent findings, new places to eat, fun places to go for family fun, dance halls, the best bars, special exhibits, upcoming local festivals called *"sagra,"* art and music performances. They are indispensable resources.

My list of superb guides for Florence amounts to one (in my humble opinion.) The finest guide I have experienced in my 40 years of traveling to Florence is Christina Mifsud. She is an art history teacher who has lived in Florence for over 30 years and is one of the few Americans who passed the tourist test. Learn more about her at her website: http://christinasflorence.com

So, strap on your well-worn walking shoes and explore this gem at your leisure with this pocket walking guide in bella Firenze.

Buon Viaggio,
   Antonia

* * *

Introduction

What to Expect

Florence is always busy. Be prepared for people at nearly every turn year-round. Getting up early is the key to enjoy this city. Like nearly every city in Italy, it is best seen on foot. Expect to walk at least 10K to 30K steps a day. Sunsets are spectacular especially if viewed from a hillside or rooftop bar. The most crowded hours are between 11 and 5. **And if at all possible, avoid the insufferably hot summer season.**

Firenze is one of the greatest treasures on Earth. It is so stunning because of the concentration of discoveries and artifacts left behind, for all of us to ponder and enjoy, of the Etruscan Age, the Medieval Ages and Gothic period, the Renaissance, Italian Mannerism and the Baroque era. Italy has more art on the planet than any other country and nearly 70% of the art is found in Florence.

This guide concentrates on modernity and the Renaissance which began in Florence in the 15th Century, largely due to the genius and support of the Medici family. The Medici largesse of intellectual and financial capital supported artists, poets, architects, scientists and politicians who left a legacy of riches that endured, and we enjoy six centuries later.

It is impossible to "see" and to "experience" all of Firenze in a few days or even a few months. Its rich history cannot be abbreviated in a few paragraphs or guidebooks. And hundreds of books have indeed been written about this one-of-a-kind city, its history, people and art. So, I will give you just **a taste of its delights hoping you will return for more.**

This is a pocket guide of five walking tours. Each walk has a theme.

Each walk is from 3 to 5 hours in duration. Each will take you to museums, gardens, artisan studios, trattorias, gelaterias or markets. Your experiences would not be complete without eating the divine Tuscan food, wine and gelato. I have included my list of favorite places to eat in Florence. There are scores of scrumptious dishes to dazzle your palate all over this fabulous city. You will also find a list of places to stay and authentic gelato shops to try.

Consider this book your appetizer to your introduction to Florence. My hope is that you will read more about her over the months and years to come and return again to explore some more. This book is a compilation of places I have personally experienced and share with you now as you walk through this stunning center of modernity, Medieval, Gothic, and Renaissance art and food. Oh, yes!……The food!

Buon divertimento! (Have fun!)

Two

Pre-Trip Planning in a Post Covid World

What to Pack

Pack light! If you can manage to pack all of your goods in one carry-on suitcase and one backpack equivalent size "bag," DO! Less is more when it comes to traveling in Italy, especially during the crowded, hot summer months navigating crowds and cobblestone streets.

Here's what I suggest you pack for a 2 to 3 week trip. Remember, you can buy just about anything you might leave behind. Dress code minimum: smart casual will allow you to get into just about every restaurant, bar, church and museum.

   3 or 4 cotton or linen tops
   1 or 2 linen or cotton dresses
   2 pairs of leggings or pants
   1 skirt
   2 pairs of broken in walking shoes
   1 pair of sandals or flip flops if you plan to go to a pool or the beach

Pre-Trip Planning in a Post Covid World

1 pajama
5 underwear and socks
2 bras
1 swimsuit
1 cross-body bag
1 reusable water bottle
1 empty duffle bag
1 flat strip of bubble wrap
1 washcloth
Prescription medicines - (in your carry on)
Charging cord for your phone or camera
For summer travelers: anti-itch cream for mosquito bites

Some places require you cover your shoulders if you are wearing tank tops or sleeveless shirts. Bring at least one top that has sleeves or ... carry a scarf in your bag that can be wrapped around your shoulders. Short shorts are not allowed in some churches. They are best left at home. In general, **dress smart casual in Florence.**

* * *

Tips To Prepare for Your Trip

My first travel tip is simple - DO NOT TRAVEL DURING THE SUMMER MONTHS. I highly recommend you travel when the crowds are at a minimum, the heat doesn't paralyze you with exhaustion, long lines are inevitable for meals and most activities, and the cost is much higher for everything! AVOID late May through mid October. Be prepared for a less than optimal experience if you opt for the summer months. For those of you who have children in school, November and

December are great months to be in Florence as the Florentines prepare for "*Natale*," (Christmas).

PREPARE YOUR ITINERARY THROUGH YOUTUBE VIDEOS, TRAVEL BOOKS, RECOMMENDATIONS FROM SOURCES YOU TRUST

Here are some helpful resources to check out to help you plan your time in Firenze, at your leisure:

Online Sites

- Girl In Florence - Georgette Jupe
- Cher Hale at Thoughtco.com
- InstantlyItaly.com

Recommended Reading to Prep, For Fun and To Get You in An Italian Mood

- La Bella Lingua by: Dianne Hales
- Mona Lisa - A Life Rediscovered by: Dianne Hales
- My Cousin the Saint by: Justin Cartanoso
- Glam Italia! How to Travel Italy: Secrets to Glamorous Travel (On a Not So Glamorous Budget) by: Corrina Cooke
- The Lives of The Artists by: Giorgio Vasari

HIRE LOCAL, LICENSED GUIDES

Support these local treasures. You will have much richer and memorable experiences with the locals who are experts and in the know. Licensed guides run about 300-400 Euro for 2.5 to 3.0 hours. This does not include a tip. Do tip if your experience has been enjoyable. NOTE: Due to Covid, tour guides were out of work for 2 years. Imagine two years without any income. Guides are in high demand after the Covid lock down. Book guides in advance as soon as you book your airline tickets.

RESERVE MUSEUM TICKETS IN ADVANCE

You will skip the lines and enjoy more space and fewer visitors in the museums. Contact your hotels to help you if you are not able to order online in advance. **The Firenze Card** is a wise purchase if you plan on being in Florence for at least 4 days and plan to visit at least 2 sites per day. You will have access to over 75 museums and tourist sites with this pass. Check out www.firenzecard.it to learn more.

MAKE DINNER RESERVATIONS IN ADVANCE

LEARN THE BASICS

It is a sign of respect to learn the basic greetings in the language of the culture you are visiting. (Good morning. Good evening. Please. Thank you. Pleased to meet you. Excuse me.)

Italians speak Italian. Yes, English is spoken but typically only in touristy areas and rarely elsewhere.

Your attempt to use Italian words like *"prego,"* (pronounced - pray go… .and translates to please and you are welcome, shows that you care about the culture you are visiting.

Bonding through language will enrich your experience. Don't worry about getting the pronunciation exact. But DO TRY! You can learn the basics on YouTube from fabulous native speakers like Francesco at Vaporetto, or have a virtual private or semi-private lesson for a small sum with a native speaker like Cinzia Ferri. Contact Cinzia through email: cinzia@instantlyitaly.com

LEARN THE ITALIAN NAMES OF THE CITIES YOU PLAN TO VISIT IN ADDITION TO FLORENCE
Signage is in Italian of course, not English.
Florence is FIRENZE;
Rome is ROMA;
Milan is MILANO;
Turin is TORINO;
Venice is VENEZIA;
Naples is NAPOLI;
Sardenia is SARDEGNA.

This is important to know so that you book your trip to the right city and avoid any confusion or angst. Look up the names of all of your points of interest. And if you are leaving Italy for another city in another European country, look it/them up. You'll need to know the Italian name to ensure you are buying a ticket to your destination and can find the correct name on the signage identifying the destinations of trains, gates in airports, etc. For example, Paris is Parigi, London is Londra, Munich is Monaco, Frankfurt is Francoforte. Do your homework.

BRING YOUR VISA CARD or ATM/DEBIT CARD to GET EURO

Use only cards that do NOT charge a transaction fee or a conversion fee. ATM machines are the most convenient way to get Euros into your pocket while in Italy.

Do NOT get cash advances inside a bank.

Do NOT exchange money at a money exchange booth or business. The rates are a rip off.

Do NOT bring traveler's cheques.

Italy's credit card machines and ATMs only accept 4 digit PINs. If you don't have one, order one.

Leave a photocopy of the front and back of your credit cards, ID and passport at home with a loved one, just in case.

CALL YOUR CREDIT CARD COMPANY

Be sure to call your credit card company in advance or go online and provide them with the dates you will be out of the country so that holds are not placed on your card(s).

LOOK FOR SPECIAL OFFERS

In this age of Covid, Italians are getting creative with offers to bring you to Italy to enjoy *"la dolce vita."* Most hotels and B&B's have not seen or had many customers, if any, for months. The region of Lazio, home to Rome, has allocated $10M Euro to pay for two free nights of lodging when you book and pay for 3 consecutive nights, making the 4th and 5th nights complimentary. https://www.italymagazine.com/.../italys-lazio-region... Of course this will change over time as traveling resumes. Prior to Covid, Italy was the most traveled to country in the EU. I doubt that will change in the post Covid world.

BRING A WATER BOTTLE - a non-disposable one, of course. I like the water bottles that contract and collapse.

BRING TWO-PRONGED PLUG-INS

Electrical current in Italy is 220 volts, unlike the U.S. which is 110. You will need a converter. Most new appliances have a converter built in, but older ones do not. Furthermore, **Italy works on a round, two-prong plug-in**. The converter, plus a plug-in, is less than $20.00 US. Two-pronged plugs without the converter are $2.00 US.

PACK A WASHCLOTH

Yes. A washcloth. Most Americans find it odd, but true, that most Italian hotels do not provide washcloths with towel sets. So, if you are accustomed to using a washcloth, pop one in your suitcase.

DO NOT PACK A HAIR DRYER

Nearly every hotel, B&B's and apartments, will provide one.

MAKE A COPY OF YOUR VACCINATION CARD

Keep it with you at all times. Save it as a "note" on your phone or in another area on your phone that does not require wifi to access. You may need proof of vaccination to enter trains, buses, museums, libraries, restaurants, and many more places. Italy is taking the virus seriously and taking measures to protect residents and visitors.

BE PREPARED WITH THE UP TO THE MINUTE COVID GUIDE-LINES

Consult the US Embassy and Italy's government site to get organized long before you leave.
   1). www.salute.gov.it- Go to the Travelers page.
   2). https://it.usembassy.gov

LEAVE YOUR FINE JEWELRY AT HOME (enough said)

PACK A SWIMSUIT

You WILL want to dip your toes in the water during the HOT summer days. REALLY! Splurge! Dive in! One life. One Chance. Florence has a fabulous gym near the Duomo with a pool and a spa. www.klab.it

The beach is not far from town for a day trip.

PLAN YOUR ITINERARY AROUND NAP TIME

If you like to set up your itinerary ahead of time, in Italy you will need to factor in some down time. Plan your day around *"pisolino"* (nap). Most of Italy shuts down from 12 to 3 to eat lunch and to nap before resuming work at 3 and closing at 7 or 8 pm. The exceptions are museums, gardens, churches and large stores in tourist towns which often remain open.

DO NOT RENT A CAR

Cars are not needed in Florence. You can walk everywhere. Downtown is a UNESCO Heritage site and only licensed cars/taxis are allowed on the streets.

Three

Getting Around in Florence

When You Arrive at the Airport in Florence

Y ou have two options. Take a taxi or take the tram to downtown Florence. The tram stops at the main train station at Santa Maria Novella.

TAXIS - **Take a taxi ONLY from a designated taxi stand.** Stand in the long line and wait your turn at the airport and train station in the areas clearly marked for taxis. The lines move quickly. It's probably one of the only types of lines in Italy that do move quickly. Do not be cajoled to hop in a taxi by a man offering you a taxi. They are hustling for work but typically not licensed to be operating a taxi. There are fixed fees from most major airports in Italy to the city center. For example, in Florence it is around 22 Euro plus 1 Euro for each suitcase.

** * ***

Tips While in Florence

MONEY

Keep just enough cash with you for your day's expenses and leave the rest in your room in a safe place. Separate your cash from your cards while in your wallets. Most hotel rooms have safes. If not, ask at the front desk to use the hotel's safe.

KEEP YOUR COINS

Italians love to accept your small bills and your coins. They also come in handy for public toilets, tipping at trattorias, turning on light machines in dark churches to shine a light on the art, and your hotel maid service will be grateful for a few coins to clean your room every day.

TIPPING

Tipping is NOT customary in Italy. Why? The service industry in Italy is a respectable and honorable profession. Hospitality is built in to the DNA of the Italians. So unlike in the US, waiting staff are not paid a minimum wage and expected to live on tips. They are paid a livable, sometimes handsome salary for their position and it is viewed and treated as a career. Most Italians do not tip. However, I have noticed that too is changing due to so many tourists tipping. It is becoming somewhat expected in some of the more metropolitan cities like Florence. I do tip when I have had excellent service. I do not leave a percentage of the bill as a tip. I leave a few coins on the table for lunches and dinners and leave the change for breakfast at Bars to express my gratitude for the service. You will notice a service charge on your bills in most restaurants. Don't be fooled in to thinking that is a built in tip for the staff. It is NOT. It is a fee for the linen cleaning.

WATER

Summers in Italia are HOT. Stay hydrated. Cool, clean, drinkable, water is available from wall fountains in Florence. It's safe. Avoid drinking from places where a sign is posted that reads *"non potabile"* = undrinkable. I suggest you bring electrolyte packets to pour in your water during the summers so that you do not get dehydrated.

BUY VINO DELLA CASA

I encourage you to always try the *"vino della casa"* (house wine) when dining in Florence. They are fabulous, not as high in alcohol content as most US wines, and inexpensive.

SKIP THE LINES AND BUY YOUR TRAIN TICKETS FROM A KIOSK IN THE STATION OR AT A TRAVEL AGENCY

In the main train terminal in Florence, the kiosks are in multiple languages, easy to operate and often less expensive than booking online or waiting in line at the station. Rarely do tickets sell out for a train ride, even during crowded summers. But, if you want to travel in assigned seats in 1st or 2nd class or book on a special train, like the *Frecciarossa* (the Red Arrow, a fast and luxurious bullet train), buy your tickets in advance, a few days prior to your train trip. Book the *Frecciarossa* when you need to travel in a hurry. This is Italy's version of a bullet train - modern, bright red, very comfortable. It is worth the extra cost and a huge time savings when TIME is so precious on your holidays. Before you board, be sure to validate your ticket in the validation machines typically near the first car of the train facing the terminal.

FIND A TOILET IN BARS

Toilets have come a long way in the last 40 years in Florence. In the 70's and 80's it was impossible to find a porcelain seat in public restrooms. Two foot postings or imprints over a hole in the floor, in a small water closet were the most common toilets which usually also required squatting. Now, toilets with seats are available but not in large supply. Carry a small pack of facial tissue with your day bag. (Just in case.) When in need of a toilet, go into a Bar, buy something to eat or drink, and ask to use the toilet. Bars are common in Italy where they serve fresh squeezed juice, coffee, wine, bottled drinks for beverages and many other items like candy, chewing gum, breakfast brioche, *"panini,"* (sandwiches) and tickets for the *"autobus or pullman,"* (buses.) Most museums offer modern toilets but the lines are usually long. Some churches offer toilets like Santa Croce and they periodically charge 1 or 2 Euro for use. Once again, hold on to your coins.

Use one of these phrases to ask for the location of the toilet:
 "Dov'è la toilette per favore?"
 "Dov'è il gabinetto?"

USE APPS FOR NO COST TEXTS AND TELEPHONE CALLS ANYWHERE IN THE WORLD

Download an app like Whattsapp to use to call or to text fellow travelers and friends back home or with you on your trip, at NO COST. The only caveat is that you need to have access to wifi i.e., a hot spot. There are plenty of hot spots in cafes to take full advantage of this easy way to communicate. The other alternative is to buy a SIM card for your smartphone and buy a one week to one month (or more) telephone plan. Contact your service provider before you leave to see what international plans they may offer.

TABLE MANNERS

Do NOT ask for butter for your bread in restaurants or trattorias. Use olive oil and salt.

DRESS CODE

"When in Rome - oopes - Florence"... Smart casual is the best way to dress in Florence. Leave behind the shorts, tanks, fanny packs and backpacks.

THE DINNER HOUR

Dine Italian style. Dinner is typically served all over Italy starting at 8. Larger cities, including Florence, are accustomed to opening as early as 6:30 or 7:00 for Americans. You will have a better experience with the locals if you dine Italian style at 8 or beyond.

PURSE MANAGEMENT

Pick pockets do gather in Florence. It's best to keep your valuables close in a cross-body bag that is kept in front of your body with a zipped top or a backpack with a zipped top, or a hidden money belt.

Do not place your purses on the sides of chairs in restaurants.

Do not put your wallet in the back pockets of your pants.

BIKE RENTALS

Electric bikes are available to rent using an app called RideMovi. Crowds make it a challenge but on the outskirts of the city it is safe and manageable. Bike riding tours are also available through tour companies if you'd prefer to get out of the city for a day.

TAKE BUS #7 to FIESOLE

Fiesole rests on the hilltop surrounding Florence. Here you will have a spectacular panoramic view of Florence, on a clear day and far away from the crowds. Fiesole is a great place for walking especially if you enjoy hills. Go to the Palazzo Pretorio. Walk behind the palazzo and you will find a marked panoramic walk along Via Belvedere, that leads to sweeping views of the hills and town. Stop by the tourist office for a map of three walks of varying difficulty. One will take you to a terrace with views of Florence along some Etruscan walls dating back to nearly 2000 BC ending at the Convento di San Francesco. A second walk is downhill to the San Domenico monastery with fabulous views along the way. Or you can take in the quarries and see where Leondaro da Vinci experimented with flight.

Four

Where to Stay

There are many choices for places to stay in and near Florence. Here is my list. I have stayed at each, they all feel very comfortable and I find the staff at each to be extraordinary. Each hotel offers a different level of comfort and extras. I suggest you check each out online and let your dreams and budget guide your choice.

My Favorite Hotels that are comfortable, affordable 3 Stars - no spas, no frills, just hang your hat and go, go go!
 Hotel Centrale; https://www.hotelcentralefirenze.it/en/
 La Scaletta; http://www.hotellascaletta.it/

My Favorite Hotels with a Rooftop Pool and Bar
 Hotel Glance; https://www.glancehotelflorence.com/
 Palazzo Guadagni; http://www.palazzoguadagni.com/

My Favorite Luxurious Hotels
 Grand Hotel Minerva; http://www.grandhotelminerva.com

The Palace; https://www.thepalacefirenze.com
Lungarno Collection; http://www.lungarnocollection.com/
Hotel Bernini; http://hotelbernini.duetorrihotels.com/en

My Favorite Hotel in Fiesole
Pensione Bencista'; https://www.bencista.com

Where to Stay

Five

An Aperitivo On A Rooftop After a Walk

There are a number of places to enjoy a glass of wine and some snacks, Italian style, after one of your walks. Early evening just before the sunset is an ideal time to grab a chair and have a drink. If your intention is to watch the sunset, go an hour early to ensure a seat.

View on Art; Via de'Medici, 6

Christina Mifsud, introduced me to this charming bar and it's become a must to stop by with friends for at least one evening before dinner for an aperitivo with a view. When you enter the lobby, walk to the elevator and take it to the 6th floor. You will walk into the bar which is the finest, relatively unknown place to get a drink with a spectacular view of the city. Indoor and outdoor seating.

Palazzo Guadagni; Piazza Santo Spirito, 9

The Palazzo Guadagni is in the fabulous, tree-lined Piazza Santo Spirito. The palazzo was built in 1505 during the Renaissance and maintains its old world charm and hospitality. The Loggia Roof Bar is very comfortable and offers stunning views of the city. This palazzo is also a favorite place to lodge while in Firenze.

La Rinascente (Department Store); Piazza della Repubblica, 4

This is a rooftop drinking hub that has been discovered due to a posting in The Rick Steves Guide book. It has been around for years, and I enjoy it! Il Bar is located on top of my favorite department store, La Rinascente, (great prices, especially on linen) in Piazza della Repubblica. You will most likely have to wait in line downstairs and then again up top after May and before October, especially to watch the sunset. But do! Prices are great. Food selection is yummy. If it's too cold, you have another option at La Rinascente, ToscaNino cocktail bar and restaurant. This is a glass ceiling restaurant with a view of the top of the Duomo. As always in this busy city, make reservations.

The Hotel Glance; Via Nazionale, 23

The Hotel Glance is in the San Lorenzo neighborhood. Here you will find the Sky Breeze rooftop pool (the pool is for guests only) and bar (open to the public) and an outdoor Lounge Bar and Urban Garden with sweeping panorama views of the city.

Six

La Famiglia – The Medici

My introduction to the Medici began with my elegant, art history teacher who began her lesson, in the Palazzo Antinori with, "Ragazzi! Today we will begin by speaking about balls." That introduction certainly caught the attention of a room full of college coeds. Of course, our talented *professoressa* was speaking about the Medici, and flashed a slide on the screen of their coat of arms….all balls. This family acquired its vast wealth through banking. Some historians attribute the balls on their crest to represent coins. Makes sense. But we will never know for sure since there does not appear to be a definitive text describing the balls. So, coins it shall be for now.

The Medici served as the primary bank for the Vatican, loaned money to hundreds of Florentine merchants, and banked money from the guilds. They acquired so much money that in today's dollars, they would be billionaires, (not simple millionaires.) But what is important about the Medici was their financial support and encouragement of the creation of art, poetry, architecture, science and so much more.

Lorenzo the Magnificent (Lorenzo de' Medici) is one of the most significant figures of Florence who had a profound affect on Italian art, politics, science and literature. Without his support, charm, keen intellect, natural networking skills, and unquenchable curiosity, we may not have ever had The David, The Last Judgment of The Sistine Chapel, The Primavera, The Cupola of the Duomo or any dome topped building anywhere outside of antiquity, the first powerful telescopes, the great palazzo's designed by Michelozzo, the thousands of works produced by the hundreds of students of The Academy like Artemisia Gentileschi. This was possible because The Medici provided living wages, art supplies, assistants, education, food and housing to artists like Michelangelo and Botticelli and others, scientific tools and supplies to Galileo, labor and building materials to support the work of architects like Michelangelo, Michelozzo and Brunelleschi. The list of what the world would have been deprived of is long and too numerous to list given that so many of the artists and thinkers Lorenzo supported financially, had lasting influences on generations that followed over the next 500 years.

Thanks to this generosity, and Lorenzo's vision for a more informed, more beautiful and peaceful society, we have this glorious art, robust, magnificent and awe-inspiring architecture and scientific discoveries which dazzle us today. The Medici line died out in 1737 but their legacy can be seen, touched and tasted today around the world, especially so in Florence.

I hope you enjoy these walks and every moment walking among so many edifices largely created by the Medici's wealth and other wealthy families they supported.

Seven

Top 5 Walks

The city itself is a masterpiece of art that pleases the eye at every turn, with its Medieval, Gothic and Renaissance architecture by geniuses like Michelozzo, Michelangelo, Arnolfo di Cambio, Giambologna and Brunelleschi. Inside the buildings you will find treasured frescoes, paintings, mosaics and sculptures, scientific discoveries by a very long list of scientists, artists, humanists, and poets including works by Ghiberti, Donatello, Gaddi, Vasari, Machiavelli, Galileo, Cimabue, Fra Angelico, Ghirlandaio, Michelangelo, Lippi, Botticelli, Masaccio, Giotto, Da Vinci, Cellini, Della Robbia, Bronzino, ancient unnamed Greek and Roman sculptors and so, so many more. (I know. That's a long list!)

I have created 5 thematic walks for you to experience the art of **some** of these remarkable Italians and the physical and natural beauty of this legendary city with some gelato on the way. Michelangelo was a sculptor, painter, poet and architect. You can see so much of his life's work in Florence. I suggest you choose one of the Michelangelo walks to get acquainted with the man and his beloved Firenze. For lovers of the outdoors, visit two gardens, each with a panoramic view of the city. For shoppers, you will find *paradiso* in two of the largest markets in Firenze with the Market walk. One market is designed for tourists and one typically visited by Florentines for daily goods. A quiet walk to San Marco Church to experience the frescoes of a priest who had an enduring influence on the Renaissance painters and more, await you on the Meet Fra Angelico and Master Ghirlandaio walk.

* * *

Follow in the Footsteps of Michelàngelo di Buonarroti - Part One

Palazzo Medici Riccardi

Firenze was Michelangelo's adopted home. He spent much of his life in Rome but he considered himself to be a Florentine. Here he flourished, first in the workshop of his master teacher, Domenico Ghirlandaio, at the tender age of 13, then as a favored "son," apprenticed to and sponsored by Lorenzo de' Medici.

Begin with a visit to the Palazzo Medici Ricardi in the heart of Florence, two blocks from the Duomo on Via Cavour 1. Michelangelo lived in the palazzo for two years. Here he created art in the small garden area of this building and in San Marco, down the street. This palazzo was designed by Michelozzo, one of the greatest architects of the Renaissance. The architecture of this magnificent palazzo was the first of its kind, elegant, perfectly proportioned, representing the age of the Renaissance. It became the style for homes among the wealthy families of Florence and in other communities, city states and European countries for the next two hundred years.

Imagine Michelangelo as a teenager, living in a home with one of the most influential families of the era, the Medici, but particularly Lorenzo de' Medici, who treated young Michelangelo like a member of his family. In these walls he met other artists, wealthy families, philosophers, men of the Church like Fra Savonarola, and developed a close relationship with Giulio, a nephew of Lorenzo, who later became Pope Clement the VII. Giulio became an important figure in Michelangelo's life and commissioned several works including the Laurentian Library which you will see as part of your next stop.

But first, after looking at the glorious courtyard, walk upstairs to see the Chapel of the Magi painted by Benozzo Gozzoli.

Fresco by Benozzo Gozzoli in the Chapel of the Magi at The Palazzo Medici Riccardi

If you ever wondered what Lorenzo or his brother, Guliano Medici looked like, you will see them here in the fresco. "A young Lorenzo il Magnifico leads the procession on a white horse, followed by his father Piero the Gouty and the family founder, Cosimo. Then come Sigismondo Pandolfo Malatesta and Galeazzo Maria Sforza, respectively lord of Rimini and Milan. After them is a procession of illustrious Florentines, such as the humanists Marsilio Ficino and the

Pulci brothers, the members of the Art Guilds and Benozzo himself. The painter can be recognized for he is looking towards the observer and for the scroll on his red hat, reading Opus Benotti." (attributed to travelingintuscany.com).

Top 5 Walks

Lorenzo il Magnifico as a boy from the Chapel of the Magi painted by Benozzo Gozzoli in the Palazzo Medici Riccardi

Walk through the chapel to the rest of the palazzo. You will get an idea of how the family lived in these rooms. You can imagine Michelangelo eating with the family, sleeping in his room with Giulio, watching, listening as guests were welcomed and greeted in the courtyard. The uppermost floor is not open to the public. Exit and turn the corner towards the central market at the rear of the palazzo and you will see your next stop.

San Lorenzo and the Medici Chapel

One block behind the Palazzo Medici Ricardi you will find the parish church of the Medici, San Lorenzo, and one of the oldest structures of the city. Michelangelo spent nine years creating the sculptures for his benefactor's tombs, at the request of the Medici Pope, Pope Clement VII, (Michelangelo's boyhood friend, Giulio Medici). The tombs are at the back of this church and known as the Medici Chapel. Look for the tomb of Giuliano in the Medici Chapel. He was Lorenzo the Magnificent's brother who was brutally assassinated in the Duomo by the Pazzi family when the consecration began during Mass. Don't miss Night and Day before your next stop to the Laurentian Library.

Night and Day, the Medici Chapel and Tomb, sculpted by Michelangelo

The Laurentian Library

While in the San Lorenzo complex, don't miss one of Michelangelo's favorite architectural projects, he worked on with delight for over 10 years, the Laurentian Library. The texts contained in this library are a collection one of the greatest treasures of humanity including Ancient Greek texts and thousands of manuscripts spanning the 12th to 16th Centuries. Thanks to the Medici, these texts have been meticulously curated and preserved. The library and all of its details, from the windows to the carved benches, the exquisite ceiling, the flooring, were all designed by the Master. This fabulous room and the Cupola of the Vatican in Rome, were Michelangelo's favorite architectural projects.

The Laurentian Library, designed by Michelangelo

Casa di Buonarroti

Fifteen minutes *"a piedi"* (by foot) from San Lorenzo, head towards Santa Croce, where you can visit a home once briefly occupied by Michelangelo called Casa di Buonarroti, now a small museum at Via Ghibellina, 70. Here he lived in one of the five structures he owned while working on the facade of the Duomo. Imagine this area bustling with chisels, dust and the smell of paints as it served as his working studios. The museum houses two of Michelangelo's earliest sculptures, The Madonna of the Stairs, which he created at the age of 15 and the Battle of the Centaurs, sculpted while just 17 years of age.

Battle of the Centaurs by Michelangelo in Casa Buonarroti

At Casa Buonarroti, there is also an extensive library of 10,000 books including letters from Michelangelo, some of his notes and sketches and some fabulous oil paintings to honor his work. One painting is of special importance. You will find an oil painting by the first woman allowed admittance to the Academy of Art, Artemisia Gentileschi, The Allegory of Inclination. "This painting depicts "Inclination," or inborn creative ability, one of the "eight Personifications" attributed to the Renaissance master. Seated on a cloud, she holds a mariner's compass and is guided by a star above, signifying his natural disposition to greatness." (Bissell, R. Ward (1999). Artemisia Gentileschi and the Authority of Art : Critical

Reading and Catalogue Raisonné)

Top 5 Walks

The Allegory of Inclination by Artemisia Gentileschi

The Bargello Museum

Not far from Casa Buonarroti as you head towards Santa Croce, you will find The Bargello Museum, formerly a prison and my favorite museum, at Via del Proconsolo, 4. You will see Michelangelo's masterpieces from different periods of his life as a painter, sculptor, architect, and poet. Visit the Michelangelo Room. Here you will find a small round piece of marble with the Virgin and her child called the Pitti Tondo. From the age of 26 to 30 years, Michelangelo was busy carving his 17 foot tall magnificent David, on display at the Academy. He managed to also save some time to carve this lovely piece during that same period.

Top 5 Walks

The Pitti Tondo by Michelangelo in the Bargello

You can see in this freeze how Michelangelo begins to carve subjects as if they will emerge and free themselves from the marble, like Mother Mary. Mother to Mother, I hear myself saying, "Hold on tight to that precious baby boy!" She is nestling him and yet distracted by Jesus's little cousin, St. John as a boy, listening to Mary read from the open book. As a mother, I resonate with this piece where Michelangelo so perfectly captures a mother's loving tenderness and at the same time, her innate fear and apprehension of what the unknown future may have in store for her precious child. Don't we all experience that mixture of emotions with our little ones? Michelangelo was so adept at capturing human emotions in his sculptures, paintings, and poetry.

Michelangelo's sculpture of Bacchus is also housed in the Bargello. I love the details of the grapes caressing his locks.

Bacchus by Michelangelo in the Bargello

His unfinished Apollo/David also lives here. Does he look familiar? We don't know if it was intended to be Apollo or David since it is unfinished. What do you think?

While you are at The Bargello, spend some time looking at Donatello's David, the first nude sculpture created in over 1000 years at the time.

David by Donatello

Donatello's David caused quite a stir in Florence at its unveiling.

Also, look for the lion holding the fleur de lis which is the symbol of Florence, called the Marzocco, and also made by marvelous Donatello. He made a copy of the original from the 1300's which was lost or perhaps tossed in to the Arno. Historians don't know the details of the loss. Donatello's Marzocco is quite large, nearly life-like and found in the Sala Dell Consigli. It was moved to The Bargello from the outside of the Palazzo Vecchio in 1855 where a copy stands today. This was a very significant symbol for Florence. In the early 1500's the Marzocco was adopted as the emblem of the Florentine soldiers who were called *"marzoccheschi,"* sons of the Marzocco. And in 1851, the first postage stamp for Tuscany featured the Marzocco, crowned.

On the back wall of this grand hall you will also find two gold leafed panels. These are the two panels presented to the leaders of Florence to choose who would create the golden doors of the Baptistery. Ghiberti won the prize over Brunelleschi who went on to design and build the grand dome of the Duomo. The priceless Ghiberti doors of the Baptistery are now housed in the Museum of Opera of Saint Maria of Fiore behind the Duomo at Piazza del Duomo, 9. (This museum is fabulous and also home to one Michelangelo's unfinished pieta' sculpture which features Michelangelo's portrait on the character of Nicodemus.)

The Bargello is one of the greatest treasures of Florence and one spot where, at a glance, you can see Michelangelo's works during his 20's, 30's and 40's. The building is also an architectural wonder and the other pieces inside are spectacular. It's a much smaller museum than the Uffizi. The Bargello is Italy's FIRST National Museum. The next stop is where you will see how the Florentines honored her favored son.

Next, walk to the Church of Santa Croce on Piazza Santa Croce. You can enter through the leather studio on the left in the rear or through the front entrance shown above. Santa Croce is one of the most important Franciscan churches in Italy. Legends abound that it was founded by St. Francis of Assisi himself.

Basilicata di Santa Croce

Michelangelo is buried here along with Machiavelli and Galileo. You may wonder why we are concluding this walk at the site of where Michelangelo is buried, since there is much more of his life to experience. Good question. This church is a rich treasure trove of art spanning four centuries for you to explore.

Basilicata di Santa Croce

It is significant because Michelangelo spent time studying Giotto's frescoes near the main altar. Giotto's infusion of emotion in the faces and in the body positions and angles of Jesus, the Disciples, followers and others, deeply inspired Michelangelo. Up until the time of Giotto, the expression of human emotions was absent (from faces) and properly proportioned bodies did not exist in art. One must look back in time, to the Ancient Greeks for life-like human expression and perfectly proportioned bodies carved in marble and made of bronze beginning in the 4th Century B.C.

Then came Giotto, over a thousand years later. Take a moment and look at Giotto's work in Santa Croce. Giotto's frescoes of St. Francis are to the right of the main altar. He understood the vast range of human emotions and captured those feelings on the faces of his subjects in the frescoes.

We know that Michelangelo not only learned from the dissections at Santo Spirito and his time in the hospital there, he learned from the artists who preceded him, like Giotto, who inspired Michelangelo to paint and sculpt human bodies with all of its imperfections and beauty. Artists and historians could easily spend countless hours here. These frescoes alone are worth a trip to Florence.

Art continues to this day in this enormous church. Leather craftsmanship lives on behind the sacristy. If you did not enter through the leather school, exit here, and spend some time watching the leather artisans at work. This is the oldest modern leather school in Florence, the Scuola del Cuoio. It began after WWII to house, employ and teach male orphans a skill after the war so they could survive and is currently housed in the old Franciscan dormitory, behind and connected to the church. As of 2021, only one of the original orphaned students is alive and still working. You are able to watch these craftsmen/women create purses, belts, wallets and more as you pass through the hall of the school.

And for those of you who are interested in St. Francis of Assisi, one of his tattered robes and belts made of rope are in a glass case near the entrance to the school located in the church's sacristy. Before you leave the church, walk to Michelangelo's tomb.

* * *

Antonia's Italy – Walking Tours of Florence

Michelangelo's Tomb in The Basilicata di Santa Croce

* * *

The tomb of Michelangelo was designed by Giorgio Vasari who wrote The Lives of the Artists. Vasari knew and appreciated the genius of Michelangelo. "Above the tomb there are three sculptures that represent the personifications of Painting, Sculpture and Architecture. These figures appear saddened by the disappearance of the great Master. But the whole of the tomb is a mixture of painting, sculpture and architecture." The works you see are "the bust of Michelangelo (work by Battista Lorenzi) decorated with statues of Architecture (work by Giovanni dell' Opera), sculpture (work by Valerio Cioli), Painting (work by Battista Lorenzi) and frescoes the work of GB Naldini." (attributed to the Tomb of Michelangelo Buonarroti, Basilica of Santa Croce, Florence - Villages of Tuscany (borghiditoscana.net)

Michelangelo died just shy of turning 89 years in Rome. His grandson, Leonardo, made arrangements for his body to be transported from Rome to his beloved Florence where he rests today.

This concludes Part One of a half day Walking in the Footsteps of Michelangelo.

* * *

Hungry?

Florence is divided into four quadrants/sections of town. Santa Croce is one of them.

Piazza Santa Croce, Photo by Vvoevale

This part of town is less expensive than the area near the Duomo and loaded with shops and cafes. The piazza in front of Santa Croce is often made into an outdoor concert venue. Fabulous musicians deliver concerts here regularly in May and June. Check out the concert schedules at your hotel. The trattoria's nearby are numerous and some offer the famous Fiorentina bistecca, 2-3 pounds of porterhouse steak for meat lovers.

I suggest Casa Toscana near Santa Croce's main piazza for lunch. If you are facing Santa Croce it is on the left. Via Giovanni Da Verrazzano, 3/5r, Tele: 055-22-60-064 - www.trattoriacasatoscana.it

I also recommend a trattoria named Finisterrae, Piazza di Santa Croce, 12 - www.finisterraefirenze.com

Both restaurants serve locals and tourists, the ingredients are fresh, flavors and aromas are bountiful, and the red house wines are full bodied Tuscan delights. After you have enjoyed *"pranzo,"* (lunch) if you are feeling up to part two, head over to Palazzo Vecchio, the current town hall of Florence located in Piazza della Signoria. If you'd rather, take a nap, pause and come back for Part Two of Walking in the Footsteps of Michelangelo di Buonarroti. This will be waiting for you.

* * *

Follow in the Footsteps of Michelangelo di Buonarroti - Part Two

Portrait of Michelangelo by Daniele da Volterra

The genesis for Michelangelo's David began at the Palazzo Vecchio with an announcement from the local governing body initiated by the Medici. It was here that a contest was shared with the people which Michelangelo heard about days later while working for the Pope in Rome. He returned to Florence and began work on The David. But more occurred here at the Palazzo Vecchio that involves Michelangelo which you will explore inside this magnificent palazzo.

Palazzo Vecchio

The Palazzo Vecchio has been at the heart of Florentine politics and economics since the 13th Century and continues to play an important role in Florentine life today. In the 1500's Michelangelo left his mark in the great hall, the *Salone dei Cinquecento*, (The Salon of 500), with a cartoon of a fresco that was once here of a famous battle scene. All of the scenes in this room you see today were pivotal to Florence's ancient successes on the battlefield in the 14th and 15th Centuries. Unfortunately, all that remains of Michelangelo's cartoon is a copy by one of his contemporaries which is not visible in the hall but is available in art history books.

The Palazzo Vecchio in Piazza Signoria

During this period of work in the massive hall of *Il Salone dei Cinquecento*, imagine Michelangelo and Leonardo contemplating their work, at the same time. Yes, these two legends graced these halls at the same time. Most likely, they were both working on their enormous cartoons. It's great fun to stand here and imagine these two Masters toying with and or ignoring each other as they worked. This room is where a lifelong discord could have easily manifested in glances or quips between Michelangelo, two decades younger, and Master Leonardo da Vinci. They admired and yet also ignored and often scorned each other. I would like to think that these two geniuses admired each other's work more so than resenting each other's talents and vastly different personalities. One can only imagine what happened in this hall as each artist attempted to create their contributions.

The Salone dei Cinquecento in the Palazzo Vecchio

Neither one of their cartoons or frescoes can be seen today, but you can imagine what they must have been like from the immense frescoes before you. Michelangelo was called back to Rome by Pope Julius II and regrettably was not able to complete his Battle of Cascina. Leonardo, true to form, experimented with paint that did not yield good results and he abandoned his efforts. Remnants of what some claim to be Leonardo's fresco were recently discovered while cleaning and restoring one of the frescoes when a false wall was discovered behind the fresco being cleaned in the great hall. Some historians believe this was Leonardo's work but as of this writing, it has not been confirmed. I suggest you take a guided tour of this palazzo to fully appreciate its significance and art treasures it holds.

What remains of Michelangelo in the Palazzo Vecchio? A nine foot unfinished statue called the Genius of Victory lives here. Michelangelo's model for the younger man of this statue, kneeling down on the back of an elder man, was a man he loved, a nobleman named Tomasso dei Cavalieri. We know Tomasso was beloved by Michelangelo through 30 poems of his collection of 300 poems, their 30 year friendship, the use of his face as a model on a number of drawings and his presence at Michelangelo's bedside when he died. Understanding his life, his relationships, will deepen your appreciation for his work and contributions we benefit from today.

The Palazzo Vecchio is also where another drama in Florence unfolded during Michelangelo's time which certainly impacted his life. A Dominican friar, Fra Girolamo Savonarola, was burned at the stake in this square just outside the palazzo in the piazza. The friar ordered the *Burning of the Vanities* (valuable works of art, paintings, books, mirrors, clothing, jewelry and other items of luxury), gathered by young boys whipped into a frenzy who broke into Florentine homes to collect these treasures on Fat Tuesday, the day before Ash Wednesday, in 1497. In his sermons, he damned and questioned the wealthy of Florence and shamed them for not taking care of the poor and having too much luxury. Fra Savonarola led to the eventual downfall of the Medici and he died, some historians believe, because he angered too many wealthy families with his sermons. He died in this piazza in 1498. There's never a dull moment in this town and that has been the case for over 800 years.

By far the most significant event that impacted Michelangelo's life as a sculptor, was initiated here at the Palazzo Vecchio where it was mentioned the contest was announced in 1501 to build a sculpture to represent the glory of Florence. Upon Michelangelo's return to Firenze, he requested an abandoned single piece of marble known as The Giant, and began work on The David, which he completed nearly three years later, as his response to the contest.

David by Michelangelo, Photo by Ravis

Now walk to The Academy to see this glorious masterpiece which has been here since 1873.

The Academy

Spend some time looking at the unfinished sculptures that line the hallway on your walk down the hall to The David. These sculptures are also carved by Michelangelo. I think they are some of his most magnificent and compelling sculptures. You can see faces and limbs emerging from the marble. If only Michelangelo had more time to completely free them. You will need to book reservations in advance. A guided tour of The Academy is recommended. There is much more than David to see in this fabulous museum, especially for those interested in sculpture.

David by Michelangelo

The David is certainly one of the most recognized monumental statues in the world. He attracts the attention and commands the awe of millions each year. Out of concern for his safety and to ensure his longevity, David was relocated from his original spot of honor in front of the Palazzo Vecchio (where you will see a replica today) and lives here at The Academy. This historic building has a deep significance dating back to the Renaissance. This was the Harvard, The Oxford of its day for artists. Admission was granted, (not necessarily earned.)

The Academy, was originally named the Arts of Drawing and founded in 1563 by Cosimo I de' Medici. In 1784 it became the Academy of Fine Arts. Music education and training, and a music museum was once in full swing here. Nearly one hundred years later, in 1873, the decision was made to move David from the Piazza Signoria to this location. For nine years, David, was in a crate, on premise, until the space was designed and created to properly fit and display him publicly in the renamed Galleria dell' Accademia. The David was released from the box and placed on his current domed pedestal in 1882 where he can be studied and admired.

What is special about David? Like most art, you can only answer that question for yourself. When you stand before this single block of Carrara marble, what thoughts do you have? What emotions do you feel?

What do we know about Michelangelo and his work on this abandoned and rejected block of marble, once called The Giant? Here are the basics:

- David represents the David of the Old Testament: a young Jewish boy, a shepherd, who bravely slew a giant named Goliath with a rock thrown from his sling, in a battle with the Philistines.
- David represents the courage, the glory, the bravery of Florence, similar to young David and his courage, heart and commitment in his battle with Goliath
- Michelangelo created David to be 17' tall
- He weighs 6 tons
- Michelangelo incorporated and was influenced by two statues at The Vatican, The Roman statue of Apollo and the Roman Torso thought to be that of Hercules.

David has been damaged by natural elements and attacked by humans. Yes. There are some stories to be told. You can look the details up online. Or for more information about the attacks and restoration, consult a guide.

Allow yourself a couple of hours to visit the entire museum. **The**

bookshop is fabulous.

***

Next, you will leave the Academy and cross the Arno on the Ponte Vecchio. Follow the signs to the Church of Santo Spirito in Piazza Santo Spirito.

But first, stop for a gelato on the way at Vivoli, Via Isola delle Stinche, 7r

Gelateria, Photo by Dario Racane

***

Now that you have seen the magnificent 17 foot tall David, you will now experience Michelangelo's exquisite wood carving in the Church of Santo Spirito across the Arno River from The Academy, which is significantly smaller than David.

The Church of Santo Spirito

The Church of Santo Spirito

Michelangelo considered himself to be a sculptor first among his many talents. When he died, many said humanity lost four great Masters, i.e., a sculptor, a painter, a poet, and an architect. Michelangelo's first love was sculpture. His finished and unfinished marbles in The Academy leave most awe struck. He also carved one piece, just one, in wood.

Wooden Crucifix carved by Michelangelo

The legend of this simple yet striking wood carving is that Michelangelo created it as a gesture of thanks to the priest who allowed him to study the human anatomy in the basement of the church as the bodies were being prepared for burial. This was all done in secret with the permission of the local priest, when Michelangelo was just 17 years old.

This period of time was a turning point for Michelangelo's development as an artist. The dissections allowed him to learn how the body works from the inside out. At the time, if these dissections of the corpses had been discovered, Michelangelo would have suffered greatly, perhaps even put to death, at the hands of the Catholic Church, especially since it was during a period of great upheaval in the city.

It is no wonder that Michelangelo's carvings featuring life-like muscles and the delicate body parts of a young man seem to be alive, suspended in the stone, and here too in wood. This crucifix is such a delicate piece. Look closely at Jesus's face. It appears as if he is sleeping softly, gently while his biceps are painfully lengthened and bulging with the burden of his emotional and physical weight on the cross. His hair is dark, curly, almost beautified, reminiscent of Michelangelo's studies of the ancient Greeks he learned about in San Marco's sculpture garden. But it is the pain free sweetness in his expression of peace and freedom from pain that is so lovely and draws you in to this piece of melancholic art.

The Crucifix was carved before The David. They are very different from each other, but what they share in common is the genius of emotion being released by the Master's hands. When I look at these two pieces, I feel a sense of the (D)divine present in both sculptures.

As you exit Santo Spirito Church, you are standing in one of the oldest neighborhoods of Firenze where many Artisans currently as in centuries passed, have their working studios. Be sure to walk around. Stop. Watch the Artisans at work. They appreciate your inquiries and curiosity. Enjoy the experience of walking in the footsteps of Michelangelo, Massaccio, Botticelli, Da Vinci and more.

Piazza Santo Spirito is lovely with its tree lined street. It offers several fine trattorias and cafes. While you are in the piazza, look for Trattoria La Casalinga at Via dei Michelozzi, 9r, +39 055 21 86 24. This has been a favorite trattoria of mine for over four decades due to the delicious Tuscan cuisine and entertaining staff. They can be a bit edgy at times, but that can be Italy. Casalinga is a favorite to the locals and *"pranzo"* (lunch) is particularly busy.

This concludes Part Two of Walking in the Footsteps of Michelangelo

There's more to see of Michelangelo in Firenze:

- Room 40 of The Uffizi is Michelangelo's room.

- Santa Maria Novella Church is where he spent hours under the

tutelage of Master Ghirlandaio.
- And San Marco is where he spent time in the sculpture garden as a young boy and witnessed the genius of Fra Angelico's frescoes.
- Below the Medici Chapel there is a recent discovery from the 1980's of charcoal drawings on the walls of a small room used by Michelangelo to hide during a political upheaval when his life was threatened. As of this writing, this room is not open to the public. Check with the San Lorenzo guides. It will eventually open.

* * *

Gardens with a View - The Boboli and The Bardini

Spending a portion of your day walking to two of the most serene places in this busy city is a treat. There are several gardens in Florence. I will be taking you to two of my favorites on this walk in the *Oltrarno* (the neighborhood beyond the Arno.) You'll begin by crossing the Ponte Vecchio and cross the Arno. Remain on the street for two short blocks until you come to the Palazzo Pitti, Piazza de' Pitti, 1, another fabulous home of the Medici family, originally constructed and financed by Luca Pitti. Pitti wanted to build a palazzo to rival the Medici Palazzo. He loathed the Medici. But, he ran out of money. The Medici bought it, completed its construction and moved here. Many have walked these halls including the Hapsburgs, the Kings of Italy and Napoleon's family. This palazzo is immense and so are its gardens. Today, over 500 gems of the Renaissance hang on its walls in the chic Palatine Gallery. You can spend a few hours walking the halls at the Pitti on another day.

Today you are going to buy a ticket to access the glorious Boboli Gardens and then walk to the Bardini Garden for a panoramic view of Firenze. You will be outdoors for the next 3 to 4 hours. The ticket office is to the far right of the palazzo as you face it. Next, walk into the courtyard and cross it to exit to access the gardens in the rear.

Before you exit the courtyard, look back over this vast space. Imagine this entire courtyard, lined so that it could be transformed into an immense pool. During the Renaissance, that's exactly what the Medici commanded. As a form of entertainment, the courtyard was not only filled with water that was about 10 ft deep, it also contained small wooden battleships, manned by men who fought mock battles with the Medici family and guests observing from the balconies above. Imagine!

Now venture out to the garden towards the Egyptian Obelisk and the enormous Ancient Roman basin. You are now standing in the amphitheater of the Pitti's Boboli Gardens. These two artifacts were moved here in 1790 from the Villa Medici in Rome. For history lovers, you are standing next to an artifact dedicated to Pharaoh Ramesses II, created during his reign in ancient Egypt, which began in 1279 BC when he was just 14 years old. He ruled Egypt for 67 years. This is the Pharaoh many scholars are inclined to accept as the Pharaoh of the Old Testament who defied Moses. So, you are standing in the presence of Ancient Egyptian History, Roman Antiquity and the Renaissance, at the same time. You are a time traveler!

Why an obelisk? The Ancient Romans developed an interest in Egypt. (Perhaps starting with Antony and Ceasar's love interest in Cleopatra.) Collecting Egyptian artifacts has long held a particular fascination to the Romans and later Italian City-States. Of course, like so many pieces of art, this obelisk was removed from Egypt after the Ancient Roman conquest, brought to Rome and then moved again to Florence, to enjoy its beauty and prestige. In the 1st through 3rd Centuries, these obelisks were shipped on three boats, tethered together and the obelisk was held in place by huge beams and held under water. Imagine how large this flotilla must have been to support these solid blocks of granite being pulled from Egpyt to the port of Ostia under water. The concentration of obelisks from Egypt is in Rome. There are more obelisks in Rome than the entire country of Egypt. This obelisk's prior location was also in Rome until it was eventually moved here to the Pitti's Boboli Gardens.

The Amphitheater and Obelisk of the Boboli Gardens at The Pitti Palazzo

The amphitheater was used as an actual outdoor theater and served as a festive venue for entertainment for over three hundred years. Now walk to the top of the stairs in front of you. You can take the stairs to the top from here and make detours through the side yards. Or you can keep walking up to the very top where you will be in a rose garden and have a view of the rolling hills behind the Pitti. You can walk, relax, or bring a picnic and rest. The gardens are for you to explore and enjoy.

The Pitti's Boboli Gardens

When you are ready, the Bardini Garden awaits. It is smaller than the Boboli and offers a cafe with refreshments and a knockout panorama of Florence. You can walk from the Boboli to the Bardini. Ask for the map when you buy your ticket at the Pitti. If you prefer, you can also take a taxi by going back to the entrance to the Pitti and ask the clerk to call a taxi for you. One might be waiting.

Statuary of the Bardini Gardens and a Sweeping Panorama of Firenze

The Bardini Garden is on top of the hill overlooking the Bardini Museum just one block off the Arno. There is a very small museum in the Bardini Villa on the property on top of the hill. Check to see what the exhibit might be. It's very pleasing to walk through this quaint villa. The mountain top Bardini Gardens, which opened up after a 12M Euro restoration in 2005, is magnificent in its natural beauty. There is a spectacular outdoor café with a sweeping view of Florence which is worth the trip and requires a refreshing drink of water or a glass of wine. If you choose to go to the Bardini before you go to the Boboli, take a taxi to the top to get to the Bardini Villa which gives you access to the gardens. It is too steep to walk. A personal favorite.

* * *

Markets! The Sant'Ambrogio and Central Market

Sant'Ambrogio Market

Begin this walk in the early morning at Piazza Lorenzo Ghiberti at the oldest market in Florence where the Florentines shop from 7am to 1pm, Sant' Ambrogio. You will not see many tourists here. It is an exceptional and also typical Italian market with traditional food, fresh fruit and produce from local farms, fresh meats and fish, a huge selection of cheeses, fresh pasta, olives, jams, wine, and cookies. You'll find household gadgets for sale, clothing, house plants and flowers. (Florentines love flowers!) I love the theme for the market, *"We are many, but one unites what unites us all: the love for good food and for Florence."* Spend an hour or more here. Grab a coffee and a pastry and listen to the sounds of the Florentines chatter and bargain.

* * *

The Central Market

Now we will walk across town to the Central Market behind the Church of San Lorenzo near the Medici Chapel in Piazza del Mercato Centrale, Via dell'Ariento. This is the old leather market of Florence and yes…you can find some great buys here. I suggest you use your duffel bag from the packing list, to bring back some of these items for holiday gifts. But beware of knock offs.

Bargaining here is expected. Most of the stalls are now run by newcomers who have made Florence their home. Many speak English. I would avoid buying any big ticket items here and focus on the belts, wallets, handbags, scarfs, wooden Pinocchios, Florentine paper and stationery. Keep your cross body bag, zipped and close to your body at all times here.

After you have shopped for your gifts for yourself and loved ones, go inside the immense building behind the stalls. This is a three story food market which was constructed in 1874. It was designed by Giovanni Mengoni who was also the architect for the Galleria Vittorio Emanuele II in Milan. This is an ideal spot to buy some fresh fruit for some snacks, or if you are cooking, your dinner items. Go to the top floor where you'll find a food court, several wine bars and a Chianti consortium where you can taste a variety of wines from the region. The food here is fantastic, very reasonably priced, and the food court is open until midnight.

This concludes our Market Walk.

* * *

Meet Fra Angelico & Michelangelo's Teacher - Master Ghirlandaio

Basilica of San Marco

Down the street from the Palazzo Medici Riccardi, you will walk to the Basilica of San Marco at Piazza San Marco, 1. San Marco is just a 2 minute walk from The Academy where you may have already visited David. The monastery of the Basilica is where you will buy your ticket to enter the inner courtyard. There is a museum off to the right of the ticket box but I suggest you see that later. For now, walk to the far right corner of the courtyard towards the bookshop and walk up the stairs to the "cells" where the Dominicans slept. Thanks to the Medici family, the church and the convent were renovated and rebuilt during the Renaissance to look like a Renaissance structure by Michelozzo, who designed Palazzo Medici Riccardi for the Medici family as their residence.

Now continue to the top of the stairs. You are in store for an image of great beauty. At the landing you will see one of the most beautiful frescoes in Florence - a fresco of The Annunciation, painted by a Dominican, Fra Angelico (Angelic Friar). He was from the Early Renaissance who earned his reputation from these frescoes in San Marco. This delicate Annunciation influenced Leonardo da Vinci's painting of the Annunciation nearly 20 years later. Leonardo was born three years after Fra Angelico died. You can see Leonardo's Annunciation in the Uffizi. You will instantly see the similarities between the two paintings. In these paintings, the Archangel Gabriel appears to the Virgin Mary to announce the conception of her son, the Son of God.

The Annunciation by Leonardo da Vinci in the Uffizi

The Annunciation by Fra Angelico in San Marco

There's more of Fra Angelico's frescoes throughout the floor. He painted a fresco in each of the little cells and each is unique. Peek inside. Imagine a bed, a desk, a candle holder in each room back when it was in use as a friary.

Now go to the far corner of the floor and you can see the cells of Fra Savonarola. He was a friend to the Medici, initially, and then, his preaching led to the demise of the Medici. Later, he was arrested, condemned, hanged and then burned at the stake in Piazza Signoria in 1498. His story? Well it's complicated. For some he was an advocate for social reforms and social justice. For others he was a radical, an extremist, a religious zealot. Read more about him to reach your conclusions.

Next, you can walk into the library, also designed by Michelozzo, on the same floor. This contains some gorgeous old manuscripts all hand painted. Walk downstairs to the bookstore for another surprise.

With your back to the cashiers in the bookstore, face the back wall. There is a very beautiful painting of The Last Supper painted by Michelangelo's teacher, Master Domenico Ghirlandaio. This is a hidden gem in Florence and absolutely stunning. Take a look at the details and the expressions of Jesus and the Disciples. Look at the folds in the drapery. This is one of my favorite paintings in Florence.

The Last Supper by Domenico Ghirlandaio

Check out the bookstore before you leave. They have a great collection of postcards.

Note: If you like Ghirlandaio, there is an additional Last Supper he painted hanging in the refectory of the Church of Ognissanti at Borgo

Ognissanti, 42 in Florence, yet another fabulous church rich with art and history.

This concludes our walk of Fra Angelico and Master Ghirlandaio

Eight

Florentine Food

Tuscan cuisine in Florence is plentiful. I have enjoyed the fabulous, fresh food at these restaurants for 40 years. The list below includes only places where I have dined repeatedly and unabashedly recommend for authentic, fresh Tuscan food. These family run *trattorias* and *ristoranti* continue to offer only the freshest ingredients. (Note: The trattorias are typically more economical than the ristoranti.) Many are well-known to locals and have become popular with tourists. All require reservations. They continue to share in common two traits: they primarily still serve locals and take enormous pride in cooking with fresh, simple ingredients that are bursting with flavor. All but Friganti are in Centro or the Oltrarno.

Some advice: There are so many restaurants in Florence. It is epicurean heaven. If you find one as you walk about, follow some basics:

- If you walk into a place to eat and the menu is in multiple languages and offers food other than Italian cuisine, leave.
- If you walk into a place to eat and there are no Italians, leave.
- The good news is that there are many fabulous places to eat in Florence. You will stumble upon them.
- Avoid the main streets.
- And, follow your nose.

Florentine Food

More advice: You are in Italy where you must eat like Italians. That means, no fast food, no butter on the table, no condiments on the table or part of the meal. It also means you do not ask for changes to the dish. You can ask for gluten free suggestions. (Italy probably offers more gluten free menus than most American cities.) Try the bread. Florentines have eaten salt free bread since the 1200's when nearby Pisa imposed a tax on salt. The Florentines refused to pay and ever since bread is made without salt. You can certainly find delicious breads in the market with salt today. But the traditional salt free bread is commonly served in many trattorias 800 years later. It is usually placed on the table and a bread charge (1 to 3 Euro per person) is typically added to most bills whether you eat it or not. And, if you don't ask for the *"il conto"* (the bill), you will wait and wait and wait some more time for the check.

Water is not served unless you ask for it. Natural and fizzy water are available typically in large bottles. You can certainly ask for natural or bubbly water. For lunch and or dinner try the house wines. Nearly every cafe, trattoria or restaurant offers *"vini della casa"* (house wines).

Each of the 20 regions offers special dishes, breads, pasta, meats, olive oil, desserts and wine unique to that region. In the Tuscan region here are some dishes enjoyed by Florentines:

Tagliere - a plate of cold cuts and cheeses

Pappardelle al Cinghiale - long, wide pasta with wild boar sauce. Heavenly!

Paglia e Fieno - hay and straw pasta, bits of guanciale, peas, pecorino cheese

Bistecca Fiorentina - a two to three inch thick porterhouse that weighs at least 2lbs

Zuppa di Fagioli Bianchi - white bean soup sprinkled with olive oil. Divine!

Pappa al Pomodoro - soup made with day old bread, tomatoes, basil, olive oil and garlic

Panzanella - salad made with tomatoes, olive oil, salt and chunks of stale bread

Salumi - a variety of salami

Finocchiona Salami - Tuscan salami with fennel

Local Focaccia

Pecorino Cheese

Ricotta di Bufala - ricotta made with buffalo milk

Lampredotto - a warm tripe sandwich

Tripa - tripe, an acquired taste, added to soups and sandwiches

Pizza - save pizza for dinner. The ovens are not heated until early evening (all over Italy)

Porchetta -fatty, boneless pork roast, roasted over a wood fire for at least 8 hours

Cantucci con Vin Santo - mini almond biscotti served with sweet Vin Santo dessert wine

Limoncello - Yes! Limoncello (a liquor made from lemons) comes from the south

Aperol Spritz - a refreshing drink has made its way from Torino to all of Italy

Gelato - deliciousness in a cup or in a cone and invented in Florence!

Note for beef lovers: The bistecca is about 2lbs (or more) a serving. Florentines like their bistecca "sangue" rare and usually bloody. You can ask it to be cooked medium. Good luck asking for it to be well done.

Nine

Top 14 Places to Eat

Trattoria Casalinga
Lunch or Dinner

Via dei Michelozzi, 9/r
www.trattoriacasaling.it
+39 055218624

This remains at the top of my favorite's list. Every pasta dish is scrumptious. Try the house wines. Near Santo Spirito Church just off the Piazza Santo Spirito. I enjoyed bowls of pasta bolognese and *"coniglio"* (rabbit) with roasted potatoes here as a student and I return here every time I visit Florence.

La Fettunta
Lunch
Via dei Neri, 72r
+39 055 2741102

Near the Palazzo Vecchio. Fantastic menu of Tuscan classics and fabulous wines. Try the *"tagliere"* (assortment of salami meats and cheese) and the herb ravioli. Very tasty dishes. Casual with comfortable seating.

Trattoria Le Mossacce
　Lunch or Dinner
　Via del Proconsolo,55r
　www.trattorialemossacce.it
　+39 055 294361

The atmosphere is hospitable and the food is delicious. Just 8 tables. Near the Bargello. Very cozy. Feels like you are being entertained in a Florentine home. The food is prepared in front of you in an open kitchen by the chef so you are readily entertained. The simple, home cooking with Chianti is absolutely delicious every visit.

La Menagere
Breakfast Lunch or Dinner
Via dei Giorni, 8r
www.lamenagere.it
+39 055 0750600

For foodies. This is not traditional Tuscan cuisine, but it is certainly Tuscan. La Menagere is an experience in a lovely setting with small plates of deliciousness. The dishes are prepared and presented as pieces of art by a young hip chef. (This is Christina's favorite place for a large yummy cappuccino.) Small plates with a fresh Italian spin on nothing but fresh ingredients.

Botteghina Cafe Pitti
Lunch or Dinner
Piazza de' Pitti, 9
+39 055 214323

Across the street from the Pitti Palace. Loads of outdoor seating. Excellent dishes with truffles and more truffles. The gnocchi with seafood is fabulous. Great spot to dine and to people watch.

Fratelli Briganti
   Lunch or Dinner
   Piazza Giovanbattista Giorgini, 12/r
   +39 055 475255

Started in 1960. Frequented by locals. Family run by the Briganti brothers and now, the second generation adult children. Must take a taxi here if you are staying in the center of town since it is on the outskirts. Excellent *"scaloppine al marsala, patate arrosto, fagioli all'olio,"* (veal scallopini marsala, roasted potatoes, and beans in olive oil).

Cantinetta Antinori
   Lunch or Simply a Glass of Antinori Wine
   Piazza degli Antinori, 3
   www.cantinetta-antinori.com
   +39 055 292234

When I was a student, our University was on the second floor of Palazzo Antinori and the Cantinetta had one purpose - to provide wine tastings for the fabulous Antinori wines. When the lease expired after 40 years, the Marchese remodeled and repurposed the Gonzaga classrooms. (Gonzaga University moved across the street from the Giardino dei Semplici, a 16th-century garden created by the Medici family.) The former classrooms now serve as the Marchese's private residence in town. The Cantinetta Antinori expanded and has become a premier, high end culinary treat to some of the finest Tuscan dishes served in the courtyard of this fabulous palazzo which also serves to support the vast Antinori viticulture and olive oil business. It is across the street from the Palazzo Strozzi.

Francesco Vini
Dinner

Borgo dei Greci 7/r
https://en.francescovini.com/
+39 055 218737

One of my favorite dishes in Italy is *"pappardelle cinghiale,"* (pappardelle pasta with wild bore) "sugo," (sauce.) I think Francesco's *pappardelle* is the best I have eaten, not just in Florence, but anywhere. This fabulous trattoria is between the Bargello and Basilica di Santa Croce.

Cinghiale - a wild bore
Quattro Leoni
Lunch or Dinner
Via dei Vellutini, 1r,
Piazza della Passera
www.4leoni.it
+39 055 218562

This is my favorite go to trattoria for a special pasta dish for pasta lovers. Of course, handmade fresh pasta is offered in just about every cafe, trattoria and restaurant in Florence. Sauces and shapes vary. But, for a heavenly pasta dish that will leave you wanting more, cross the other side of the Arno to the Oltr'arno where you will find Quattro Leoni near the Palazzo Pitti. This fabulous Tuscan trattoria is memorable. Order the *"fiocchetti - pere e taleggio."* This is a pasta that is filled with a pear stuffing, pear flakes and served with a cheese sauce and asparagus bites. Heavenly!

Antico Noe
   Lunch or Dinner
   Volta di San Piero, 6r
   www.anticonoe.com
   +39 055 2340838

Not only do the men at the Noe make the greatest sandwiches in the wine bar of this locale, the Trattoria serves up authentic and equally delicious Tuscan dishes to only 10 tables next door. The Trattoria located in an antique butcher shop, in the Santa Croce neighborhood, has a large menu with all local dishes. The clientele is strictly local and Massimo and Stefano make wonderful hosts. Don't let the "sketchy" people in the area stop you from dining here. (Described by Christina Mifsud.)

* * *

Amicizia with Francesco and Mildie

Pandemonio di Casa Brogi
   Address: Via del Leone, 50r
   Quarter: Oltr'arno – Piazza Tasso
   www.trattoriapandemonio.it
   +39 055 224002

This restaurant, located in the Oltrarno, has a lovely trellised garden area for relaxed outdoor summer meals. Since 1992, this family run restaurant is known for its fish dishes. The fish platter (both shell and non-shell fish) served in a large metal skillet, loaded with pieces of Tuscan bread, is the most delectable (Described by Christina Mifsud).

Mercato Centrale
   Lunch or Dinner

Piazza del Mercato Centrale
Via dell'Ariento
www.mercatocentrale.it

Go to the top floor where you will find a food court with a lot of variety and bars for wine tasting. The top floor closes at midnight.

Al Antico Vinaio
Via dei Neri, 65r
www.allanticovinaio.com
Best Go to Place for Sandwiches (Panini)

Florentines make fabulous sandwiches. My girlfriend, who has two teenage daughters, who love panini for a good price, told me about this place 2 minutes from the Uffizi. It was not around 40 years ago. Self serve cafeteria style dining was the rage then. Al Antico Vinaio is as the Italians say, *"da morire"* (to die for.) They make the best sandwiches I have tasted in Florence. And the price is right…around 7 Euro for a huge portion of deliciousness. It's worth the wait! No seating. Best to get in line, then take your sandwich to an outdoor bench nearby or to your hotel.

Photo by Rosshelen

Cibreo Trattoria
   Via del Macci, 122r
   Across the street from the Ambrogio Market.

Not to be confused with the other three Cibreo in Florence, the Trattoria is traditional Tuscan food for the right price. Cibreo Ristorante and Cibreo Cafe are also a treat but I prefer the Cibreao Trattoria since locals still dine here. I could eat platefuls of the chicken and ricotta meatballs. They are known for the veal tripe salad which reminds me of a dish my Nonnie would have relished. The flourless chocolate cake is divine.

Photo by Susan Yan

Buon Appetito!

Ten

Top 4 Authentic Artisanal Gelato Shops

Gelato is not ice cream. Heavy cream and fresh fruit make it so very delicious. Thanks to Catherine de Medici commissioning Bernardo Buontalenti to prepare a dinner for the King of Spain, gelato, as we know it today, was created in the 1500's.

I have four favorite spots in Centro in Florence where I know the ingredients are fresh and made onsite daily. Avoid gelato shops where the gelato is brightly colored (it's not fresh) or stacked high. Ask if the gelato is made daily. That's essential. If not, choose another. There is no comparison between fresh and manufactured gelato. Here are my favorites.

Vivoli
Via Isole delle Stinche, 7R
Opened in 1929

Perche' No!
Via dei Tavolini, 19r
Opened in 1939

Gelateria dei Neri
Via dei Neri, 9

Open for over 30 years

Gelateria Della Passera
Via Toscanella, 15R
Opened in 1939

Delizioso!

Eleven

Grazie Mille!

Ciao a tutti! This is my first effort writing a book. It's been so much fun sharing my second home with you. There's more to come. Look for more of Antonia's Italy - Walking Tours in a few months. I hope this guide provided you with some fun facts and delivered some adventures that will leave you with warm feelings and a full belly of delicious Tuscan cooking and sweets.

Twelve

Let's Hear From You!

Thank you for exploring Firenze with me! I know the choices for pocket guides are plentiful. You can help spread the word that Florence is a fabulous place to experience by leaving a review of this book on Amazon or IngramSpark. **Thank you in advance for doing so!**

Feel free to reach out to me with your comments: antoniasitalywalkingtours@gmail.com

Buon Viaggio!

A presto!

Thirteen

Resources

https://www.italymagazine.com

https://www.therooftopguide.com

www.wikipedia.com

https://www.visitflorence.com/florence-museums/bardini-gardens.html

https://www.feelflorence.it

www.tripsavvy.com

https://www.commune.signa.fi.it

https://borghiditosanca.net

Resources

https://www.thegalleriaaccademiafirenze.it

https://www.thecollector.com

https://www.visitflorence.com/florence-museums/bardini-gardens.html

https://mercatosantambrogio.it

About the Author

Antonia Accili is passionate about sharing her experiences, knowledge and travel recommendations to those heading to the land of her ancestors, Italy. Antonia's Italy - Walking Tours of Florence is the first book she has published. Antonia studied as an undergraduate her junior year at Gonzaga University in Florence and fell in love with the majesty of this city and its people. She lives in San Rafael, CA with her husband, Jim and pup Lily. Antonia is busy drafting additional Antonia's Italy Walking Tour pocket guides for other towns in Italy including Orvieto, Lucca, Bologna, Torino, Roma, Sulmona, the island of Sardegna and more, to reveal their hidden gems - "a presto!"

Made in the USA
Las Vegas, NV
03 March 2023

68466309R00068